I0330603

Pleasant Surprises

Pleasant Surprises

INSPIRING RHYMES FOR SPECIAL TIMES

Oscar Nordstrom

North Stream Publishing

Pleasant Surprises: Inspiring Rhymes for Special Times

Copyright © 2017 by Oscar R. Nordstrom

All rights reserved.

No part of this book may be reproduced in any form or by any means, electronic or mechanical, except by a reviewer who may quote brief passages in a review to be printed in a magazine, newspaper, or on the Internet – without permission in writing from the publisher.

Although the author and publisher have made every effort to ensure the accuracy and completeness of information contained in this book, we assume no responsibility for errors, inaccuracies, omissions, or inconsistencies herein. Any slights of people, places, or organizations are purely unintentional.

Publication date: November, 2017

ISBN: 978-0-9983109-2-3

Manufactured in the United States of America

Interior and Cover Design by Foley Square Books

foleysquarebooks.com

North Stream Publishing ● 36 Thiells Mt. Ivy Rd.

Pomona, NY 10970

EMAIL: info@northstreampublishing.com

www.northstreampublishing.com

Dear _____ ,

This is a special Gift for you on the occasion of
_____ ,

I hope you enjoy it!
_____
_____
_____
_____

Signed,

_____

Holidays

SCHWINN PHANTOM

Oh how it was, so long ago,
And yet so newly fresh
A young boy's dream, on zephyr wings
Schwinn Phantom, bicycle's best

Balloon white walls on chrome spoked rims
Chrome fenders all were stock
Front wheel shocks to smooth the ride
And a built-in turned wheel lock

It had it all, a boy could want
A light, a horn, a seat on springs
A kick stand and handlebar grips
And a rear rack to carry things

Bicycle's crème de la crème
And Harley's next of kin
All chrome and lacquered paint
It called – let's take a spin

Christmas Tide

Fall ushers school, cool days, early night falls,
Cloudless skies, birds fly, sweaters and football
Leaves flare off and blanket the ground,
Harvests, pumpkins, legends abound
Red cheeks, frosty breaths, ski and skate,
Macy's, mom's turkey, we all overate
Poinsettia, wreaths, hearth and home,
The smell of pine trees, bough and cone
Egg-nog, cider, the urge to bake,
Ginger bread, spice, another fruitcake?
Holly berry, and candle glow,
Kisses under the mistletoe

Trim the tree, bright City lights,
Carolers singing Silent Night
Shoppers scurrying to and fro,
Bundles falling in the snow
Store Santa's pail & ringing bell,
TV, commercials, oversell
Icy patches, mail in batches,
Mall sales, early bird catches
Shoveling snow and winter blow,
Praying to ease the traffic flow
Frosty, Rudolph, now the Grinch too,
Every year it's something new
Dickens' Scrooge and Wonderful Life
Old favorites, a cozy respite
Radio City, Nutcracker ballet,
Department store windows, dazzling display
Santa, his sleigh and eight reindeer,
Children, sleepless for him to appear
The birth of a Savior, renewed each year
Revelers, hearty and full of good cheer,
Auld Lang Sein and Happy New Year
What's there left for us to say,
Happy Holidays all, and to all a good day!

CHRISTMAS MAKES CHILDREN OF US ALL

Christmas makes children of us all,
Whatever age, station or call
What is it though to touch our heart,
And make this day to stand apart?

The story starts as many do
A mother's term now nearly due
But something magic will descend
To change the world and time suspend

While many years have passed away
It's all renewed this very day
An infant child is humbly born
To raise the hopes of all forlorn

The radiance of this lone event
Transcends all else that's Heaven-sent
And takes us back within our heart
And like the Magi play some part

So if we truly can do that
It is not hard to reach way back
And touch the child within us still
And feel again the Christmas thrill

TO WIN A HEART

To win a heart, where shall I start,
What words of love can I impart
To steal her heart, as she has mine,
And make of mine her Valentine?

To start, the planets must align
On this my fate I must resign
For tightly kept her heart is closed,
To all those who would dare suppose

And truth to tell, I know no spark,
To kindle love her doubting heart
As locked it is by worldly plight,
And vigil kept upon the night

But try I must with Cupid's dart,
To find a way to pierce her heart
For now my love must simply bide
And wait the turning of the tide

And hope one day love comes ashore,
That I may wade for evermore
And swim in sun and wind and rain,
If only should her heart so deign

SPRING

What is there to spring's embrace
A gentle breeze upon the face
And sunny skies to brighten day,
And fields that call to run and play

Of crocus bloom, and morning dove
All life renewed, of hearts in love,
The scent of earth and outdoor grill,
Ants at work, and baseball's thrill

Park walks to stroll, as beaches wait,
And dress takes on its fashion plate
And smiling faces, commonplace,
And dining out becomes a fete

Thoughts of love are newly fetched,
And moonlight couples' lips to mesh
And tunes appear upon the tongue,
With words of love so softly sung

So what is there so loves the spring
And calls to fond remembering?
Its winter's snow and cold and sting,
That gives the magic to the Spring

Love

A NEW LOVE SONG

A songbird on one magic day,
Alit, and stole my heart away
And carried such a lilting tune,
That cast a spell upon the Moon

And suddenly my heart was gone,
She took it to a place of song,
Where polka dotted dreams are born,
And hearts unfretted to perform

Without my heart, I could not be,
So went to seek its revelry,
And give it voice in measured rhyme
To touch her heart, as she had mine

And there I found my heart reborn
To sing again its own sweet song
But should a duet come to be,
O, let it be love's melody!

And if two hearts do not agree
To sing love's song in harmony,
Let each then seek its own delight
And sing as brightly as it might

SANDRO'S LOVE

From seventh from the Sun,
His manliness cast upon the Sea
Gave birth to Virgin Beauty,
Love's visage divinely spun

Whose Golden locks do spill and flow,
For modesty and Zephyr's play,
While graced nape and supple limb,
In tender pose bestow

A chin and lips of such,
To beckon man's first kiss,
While line and cast of nose
And eyes, his soul delighting touch,

An oval face and perfect brow
Enchantment so complete,
To hide the moon and stars in shame,
Dimmed by love's endowed

While mortals stare, inspired awe,
Hearts lost beyond reprieve,
Who gaze upon in dream lost revelry,
Must live by love's implore

RENDEZVOUS

I wondered what will come to be,
When we get past all pleasantry
And will we find romance and bliss,
And seal the deal, with love's first kiss?

For, at first blush, we seemed well matched
Two souls at ease, and unattached
Two hearts and minds of kindred ken,
Cascading thoughts to each commend

And here we are, and finely met
Our eyes on each now firmly set
And dreams of finding love anew
Brought each to make this rendezvous

THE TIP OF THE ICEBERG

Why did I seek to show her more
Than she showed me of what's in store?
She saved her words, while I did not,
And told her everything I'd thought

I reached for her, but pushed away,
The very thing I sought to stay
I showed her much, but she did not
And said let time define our lot

Too late I saw what she had meant,
And tried to tell of love she'd dreamt
It's not about the part that shows,
It's all the rest, that's undisclosed

This tale if woe is sadly true
So lest the same, befall to you
In love, the myst'ry of the new
Must coalesce, like drops of dew

So should you find love comes your way
Don't ever let your words betray
Your heart, but show it day by day
And in the end her heart will sway

ALONE

I woke, and found I could not sleep,
For thoughts of her just would not keep
Alone I lay within the night,
And wished to hold my heart's delight

But she was not within my reach,
And out of sight and ear or speech
I wished to call and say goodnight,
Her voice alone would quell the bite

For surely she would understand,
She knew how well the heart commands
But waken her I could not do,
And so I wrote of love, anew

If I could find the string of words,
The sum of which her dreams have heard
I know they'd roll aside that stone,
And ne'er again I'd sleep alone

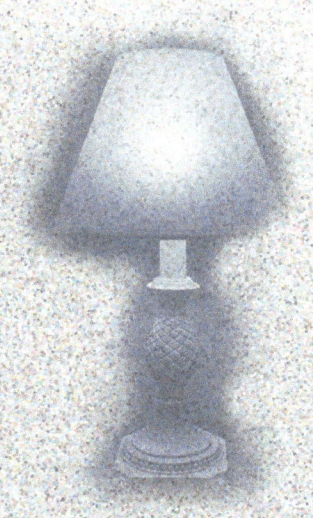

IF I CLOSE MY EYES

If I close my eyes,
I can taste your mouth and smell your skin

If I close my eyes,
I can caress your face and dimpled chin

If I close my eyes,
I can you hear your soft voice and lilting reach

If I close my eyes,
I can sense your soul and span the breach

If I close my eyes,
I can embrace you in my arms anew

If I close my eyes,
All these things I know are true,
But only if you close yours too

JUST HELLO

Just Hello, that's all she said,
But into this much more was read
She called, and that was everything,
To hear her voice and its sweet ring

Just Hello, and nothing more,
But then, no one was keeping score
One word's enough to burst a dam,
The heart hears but its own command

Just hello, an everyday sound,
Nothing's there that's so profound
Then why so much to fuss and cry?
She said hello, and not goodbye

Poems in the Key of Life

ROAD SIGNS

Life's a one-way Highway,
With markers pacing time
We are but its travelers
Passing posted signs

    Some follow after others,
    Some go a different way
    The destination's all the same
    Regardless of the stay

        Some watch the wear and tear
        While speeders pay a fine
        We all arrive at some point
        So why not stay in line?

            Sometimes the roadway merges
            And travelers come to pair
            The bumps and curves get smoother
            When two can share the wear

                When starting out the journey
                The distance seemed so long
                But as we pass each road sign
                We wonder where it's gone

MEMORIES

An open court, from far away
I heard the music softly play
Its tune recalled a bygone time
But carried in a key of gray

White sunlit drenched, a garden wall
Its quiet did my heart enthrall
And smiling eyes did greet the day
While shadows crept, and cast a pall

In winding paths, with flowers strewn
While dew dripped down a sweet perfume
And beckoned to another day
But in its scent, a mist of gloom

In rich color, did weave a spell
And cast it down a wishing well
And echoed back a sound so sweet
While tears tolled out in mournful knell

WHEN I'M NO LONGER WITH YOU

When I'm no longer with you
When I'm no longer here
Do not think I've left you
For I am always near

If you close your eyes you'll see me
If you listen, my voice you'll hear
You'll know I haven't left you
No need to shed a tear

But should you grow short sighted
And wish I would appear
Then recall the love and laughter
And drink a cup of cheer

You see I didn't leave you
And I'm not really gone
I've simply crossed the finish line
And passed on the baton

Recall when I lost loved ones
And how I carried on
Now put yourself in my place
And you'll know I haven't gone

THE OLD MAN

His face and clothes the worse for wear
I watched him, trying not to stare
But something stirred me deep inside
And called for me some time to bide

I saw the years had not been kind
Stooped, he dragged a foot behind
His step unsure, and head cast down
His eyes affixed upon the ground

Whatever reason I can't tell
I had to stop to wish him well
And as he rose his head to see
Who greeted him, it came to me

For there reflected in his eyes
I saw myself becoming nigh
And with that years did melt away
And there I saw a boy at play

So now instead of one who's old
I see someone once young and bold
And those who pose a youthful scene
I see instead an old man's mien

YESTERDAY

Yesterday sweet, and bitter hid
So ready to the present bid
But dry and sere would be the well,
Were todays but captives to its spell

Todays yesterdays soon become,
So what we do, or not, is done
No chance of recall once its past,
The die of day is coldly cast

But dwell you might upon this truth,
We lived todays upon our youth
When time was slow and all was new
With all the world before to view

Youth be not wasted on the young,
As age and sage so often sung
The waste is when we spend today,
In wistful dreams of yesterday

MY FATHER'S SHOES

From the time I could remember
My dad was always there
To lend a hand or fix something
We always knew he cared

He had a tool for everything
And knew to use them well
A handyman par excellance
Amid smoke from a Pall Mall

I never heard him rue his lot
Or utter a complaint
But he could loose a curse or two
He wasn't quite a saint

It seemed he worked, all of the time
With many mouths to fill
And it was hell to wake him up
It took a fire drill

His only fun a game of cards
All-nighters were the rule
Perked coffee pots and smoke-filled rooms
And penny ante pools

And when it was his time to go
He left without a tear
But we were all the lesser ones
You see he had no peer

And this I know I can't repay
The debt I owe today
All I can do is pay my dues
As none can fill my father's shoes

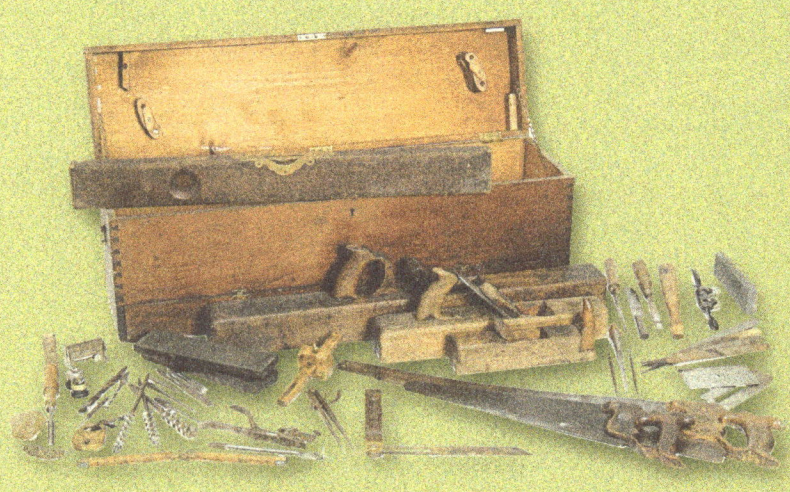

Muses

MOON'S TOUCH

One Night I gazed upon the Moon,
And thought

So many before had done the same,
And sought

To send the same to me,
Now gone

I feel their touch,
And pass it on

THE BEST THINGS IN LIFE

The aroma of fresh coffee, and its wake-up zest
The smell of a baker's oven, and rolls too hot to test
The sight of sunlight dancing, upon a rippling brook
Ivy climbing an old stone house, with slate roof edges chipped

The deafening roar jet engines make, as runways they alight
The silence of a heavy snow, upon a wintry night
The linger of a new car scent, and pleasure it entails
The thrill to find that perfect fit, and catching it on sale

The sleepy sound of rain tapping, upon a window pane
The thunder of waves crashing, along the coast of Maine
The smell of puddles drying up, after a sun-drenched rain
The pungent odor of asphalt, on newly paved road lanes

The serenity that's beckoned, by unkempt fieldstone walls
The stillness of a wooded trail, as leaves begin to fall
The sun at days end going down, against a crimson sky
A full moon climbing to the stars, a lover's lullaby

The smell of newly cut grass in spring, and musty leaves in fall
The scent of pine at Christmas time, and memories they recall
The memory of a first date, and the fear it was to face
The thrill of that first stolen kiss, and longing for its taste

The laughter of a new born child, against its mother's breast
The cooing of a morning Dove, awakened from its nest
A reading chair, a snugly nook, a favorite reading planned
A loved pet lying underfoot, or purring at your hand

A quiet time to reminisce, in memory's cobwebbed hall
And of life's woes in retrospect, it's worth it all in all

DREAMS

A world without substance, in permanent twilight
Is fed without a conscious thought, or sense of wrong or right

A glimpse of this striking world, is all that we can see
Odd visions for us to ponder, locked doors without a key

A place without set boundaries, twixt the heavens and the earth
Where yesterdays and years relived, in called upon rebirth

Old friends and long gone loved ones too, may suddenly appear
A visit from another world, with those we still hold dear

Sometimes we glimpse tomorrows, yet mixed with yesterdays
Like an old-time B grade movie, the plot the current craze

Perhaps the watch retired, when master's fast asleep,
Freed, the child can run amok, and play at hide and seek

While answers we deem valid, are hatched out in the day,
May only be old knee jerks, or tapes we've learned to play

Yet when daily thoughts coalesce and simply just won't keep
May come back to remind us what we sow we reap

At times confounding symbols, at times so very clear
Call upon reflection, or facing down our fears

Unafraid of human judgments, there's so much they can teach
If we could understand the dialect they speak

And in the end the answers there, unsettling as it seems
A truer sense of who we are, may appear within our dreams

THE TIDAL BORE

Here it is rushing, up upon the shore
It overlaps its habitat, and surges on for more
This senseless and unfeeling thing, this the Tidal Bore

And here it is receding, back from coast and shore
The very force that feeds it, now bleeds it, to whence it was before
This senseless and unfeeling thing, this the Tidal Bore

And when it's at its' ebb, and quiet seas and shore
It's just resting, biding cresting, the call for an encore
This senseless and unfeeling thing, this the Tidal Bore

And when shall earth be free, of all this constant draw
And once and all unending call, of unforgiving lore
This senseless and unfeeling thing, this the Tidal Bore

Lo, not for rest or cease, to be soon time in store
For man's estate and not moon's wake, is what to underscore
This senseless and unfeeling thing, this the Tidal Bore

THE WATER OF LIFE

Deep within the well
The water's cool and calm
The bucket splashes in
The water withdrawn

Drink deeply and long
The water gives life
Feel it spread to every pore,
And feel your heart alight

For the water of life is love

JOY

Without darkness, so love the light
And wait sunrise, upon the night?
Without the Moon, who'd play off the Sun
And chase the tides, and make them run?

Without the winter, how welcome spring?
And each new year a new beginning?
Without the cold, who'd relish warm
And pluck to brave life's wintry storms?

Without the low, where'd high be found
And who would take the middle ground?
Without the din, where'd quiet be
And who would then to keep low key?

Without the loss, where'd be the gain?
And all things tie, who'd suffer pain?
With naught to fear, who'd courage call
And conscience make of cowards all?

Without the child, who'd parents be
Each to other necessity?
Without the old, where'd be the new
And perspective to all points of view?

Without sure death, how precious life
And measure to all daily strife?
Without the hurt, who'd well employ?
Without sorrow, who'd know of Joy?

MAGICAL WORDS

"Words and magic were in the beginning one and the same thing, and even today words retain much of their magical power." — Sigmund Freud

Before the time that man could speak,
Thoughts were chained by grunt and shriek
Or scratched in dirt, or as a scrawl,
Or drawn with charcoal on a wall

With no clear way to thoughts convey
We only lived from day to day
When somehow out of time and space
An image, sound began to trace

At first, so simple yet profound
A picture painted by a sound
And thoughts now shared by word of mouth
Expanded minds by leap and bound

True magic then our words create,
To stir the heart, or make it quake
A gift and curse to man's domain,
A world of words for well or bane

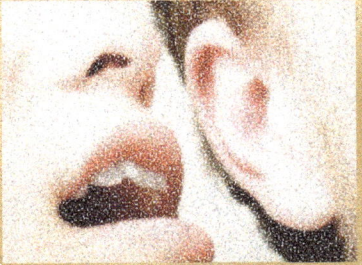
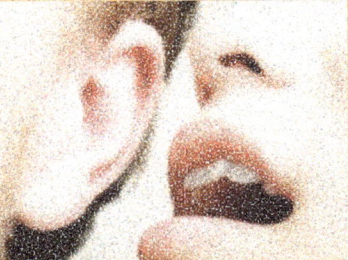

THE SELF-MADE MAN

Into a place of humbler things
Strode a man with gold-studded rings
Dressed to the nines, and sporting tan
Proclaimed to all, a self-made man

His words contained a boastful ring
"No one gave me a single thing,
I earned my place, by my command"
No chance of fate, this self-made man

No one could doubt a word he said,
He stood so far above their heads
He'd come so far, so short a span,
This self-proclaimed and self-made man

One wondered was he born of man,
Or came full grown, by his own hand
Some self-fulfilling master plan
Not childhood grown, this self-made man

One pondered too, upon his youth
Of how'd he come to learn the truth
And at what age his school began
This self-taught whiz, this self-made man

One might have thought the wealth he'd made,
Had not come by loan or trade
Perhaps some new installment plan,
Or self-coined mint, this self-made man?

One wondered too, who'd manned the gate,
While he amassed his vast estate
And had not he a Motherland,
This one man show and self-made man?

Now sadly dawned, he'd never see
No man's an isle, nor could one be
He built upon what others plan
There's no such thing as a self-made man

ILLUSIONS

Moonbeams bouncing off rippling flows,
make the running tide alive
Shadows casting ghostly forms,
unconsciously contrived
Dreams summon images,
and project fantastic scenes
Like a silent movie picture film,
exaggerating everything
Love can be an illusion too,
painting things we wish to be,
But like a mirror it can reflect,
but never does it see

A NEW OLYMPUS

I gazed up at the stars one night,
But full moon blocked their glow from sight
While stars will light a moonless sky,
This glow did heaven's course deny

For there beheld on earthly plane,
New stars did mark a newer reign
A man-made sky, dark shapes and bright,
Black outlines and beads of light

And soaring to Olympian height,
Stone cast idols to man's new rite
Unseen by all, when first begun,
Now vie to nature's perch undone

And so for all the seeming blight,
Man created much new delight
To charm the eye and lift the heart,
With form and light, true modern art

HELLO - GOODBYE

Hello . . .

Once past, time is all alike
Yesterday, last year, my youth
Seem all as one

My mind's eye pictures long-gone events
With the same rich color as those
Only just now out of sight

A friend long dead, a loving parent's look
Warm my heart as if only just now seen

. . . Goodbye

THE SEA

All hail the goddess of the sea,
That deep, mysterious deity
Whose waters gave to life its start,
And lore to muse a poet's heart

Her tides bear passion's ebb and flow
And clouds to make the rain to sow
A quiet shoal in times of rest,
But tempest tossed, when mood possessed

Who sail within her swirling mist,
To taste her salt, a sailor's kiss
Must first obey her beck and call,
Or risk to chance a sudden squall

So humbly pray for leave to sail,
On tack against the winds prevail
For those who run before her main,
May break and sink should she disdain

And all who'd flout the sea's demand
And currents under her command
May dash all hope of making land
And cry her name in foam and sand

CLOUDS

Formless, flowing, ever changing,
Childhood visions, never aging
Teasing, playful, hiding shapes
Daydreams calling, come escape

Magical fantasies, cast in white,
Soaring, sailing, vaporous kites
Fairytale castles, banners fly
Fields of white flowers, dotting the sky

Tall masted ships, sail a blue sea
File past in review, leisurely
Fair sky or foul, a sailor's friend,
Delight or warn, the weather's trend

Hide and seek, with moon and sun
Gliding shadows, patch and run
All Hollows Eve, a witch on her broom
Mount to the sky, and cast the full moon

Dampening moods, in shades of gray
Parting to chase the blues away
After the storm, rainbow delight
Brighten the day, and color twilight

Dark ominous and foreboding
Clouds turn black, white surf exploding
Thunder, lightning, drenching rain,
Rivers flooding, raising Cain

Gentle showers or wintry blow,
Life-giving potion, on earth bestow
Dreadful tempest or blissful dream
Each day brings a new regime

THE LOWLY ONION

I'm not sure, but would like to think
When nature made an onion stink
And cause the eyes to tear and blink
It did it with a nod and wink

Why else on earth would this be done
Except to have a little fun
So unsuspecting noses run
And shy away from tasting one

Yet once one gets beyond all that
And add it to a dish that's flat
It will to lifeless taste combat
And cause gourmets to doff their hat

And so it now all seems to me
That culinary pedigrees
Are not all they're cracked up to be
The onion's just as savory

And though not much upon its own
Daresay it's found in every home
And while to flavor others loan
Deserves high praise all on its own

Now I to end these lines decree:
Who hold their nose are cowardly
The onion is no wannabe
It's earned gustation's PhD

CROSSWORD PUZZLE

Words running here and there

And places intertwine

Clues and hints of every sort

And letters to combine

Fill each blank, some you guess

Let the theme define

And when it's done, it's all in fun

And intellects refine

REFLECTIONS

"Intellect is a Gift" – It's a tool that allows us to appreciate the other gifts of life, more fully.

"Imagination is a Great Gift" – It allows us to see without our eyes, hear without or ears, and feel without touching.

"Love is a Great Gift" – and the greatest of all virtues. It gives and asks nothing in return, and empathize w/o being.

"Faith is a Great Gift" – It is not a sense, but rather a connection of our being to something outside ourselves, and larger.

"Life is the Greatest Gift" – when we consider all the possibilities out of time and space, from the rise of humankind to the present moment, and all the billions of people who have lived, and the countless number of eggs and sperms that have vied for life, the coming together of two unique cells that became you, is to have hit a lottery of unimaginable odds. In fact, it is one chance in eternity.

When life serves up a compliment, take it like salt; when life serves up ridicule, take it for what it's worth.

When life serves up joy, rejoice; when life serves up tears, let them flow.

When life serves up grace, be amazed; when life serves up anger, view it as a temptation.

When life serves up beauty, behold it; when life serves up ugliness, use the other eye.

When life serves up good fortune, count your blessings; ... woe, do the same.

When life serves up peace of mind, pat yourself; when life serves up a tempest, serve it like tea.

When life serves up a song, give it voice; when life serves up noise, give it a deaf ear.

When life serves up love, let it flow without measure; when life serves up hate, return the package, unopened.

How Shall I Live?

Live as a young child with bright wonder-filled eyes. When in doubt, do what a child would do to make a good father smile. If you should fail, but persist, would a loving father require perfection? Is not the fervent try more important?

Oscar R. Nordstrom is the author of the critically acclaimed *Fountain of Change: How the Life and Ideas of Jesus Reshaped Our World*. He is the recipient of numerous awards and testimonials. Oscar is a longtime devoted scholar, author, and poet Pleasant Surprises is a collection of many of his poems and verses written over the years, following the death of his wife Susan Fay, to whom this work is dedicated. Nordstrom is the owner of a contracting and consulting firm and lives in Congers, New York.

BIRTHDAY Fathers Day Friendship New Baby Sympathy Mothers CHRISTMAS BIRTHDAY Fathers Day Friendship New Baby Sympathy Mothers CHRISTMAS HELLO! Hanukkah Wedding Anniversary Valentine Day HELLO! Hanukkah New Sympathy Mothers CHRISTMAS BIRTHDAY Fathers

BIRTHDAY Fathers Day Hanukkah *Friendship* New Baby Sympathy Mothers Wedding Anniversary Valentine HELLO! Hanukkah Sympathy Mothers CHRISTMAS BIRTHDAY Fathers Day

www.ingramcontent.com/pod-product-compliance
Lightning Source LLC
Chambersburg PA
CBHW041124300426
44113CB00002B/54